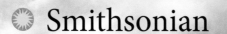
Smithsonian

LITTLE EXPLORER

WOOLLY MAMMOTH

by Kathryn Clay

CAPSTONE PRESS
a capstone imprint

Little Explorer is published by Capstone Press,
1710 Roe Crest Drive, North Mankato, Minnesota 56003
www.mycapstone.com

Library of Congress Cataloging-in-Publication Data
Names: Clay, Kathryn, author.
Title: Woolly mammoth / by Kathryn Clay.
Description: North Mankato, Minnesota : Capstone Press, a
Capstone imprint, [2018] | Series: Smithsonian little explorer. Little
paleontologist | Audience: Ages 5–9. | Audience: K to grade 3. |
Includes index.
Identifiers: LCCN 2017040840 (print) | LCCN 2017048003 (ebook)
| ISBN 9781543505498 (eBook PDF) | ISBN 9781543505412 (library
binding) | ISBN 9781543505450 (paperback)
Subjects: LCSH: Woolly mammoth—Juvenile literature.
Classification: LCC QE882.P8 (ebook) | LCC QE882.P8 C53 2018
(print) | DDC 569/.67—dc23
LC record available at https://lccn.loc.gov/2017040840

Editorial Credits
Michelle Hasselius, editor; Heidi Thompson, designer;
Eric Gohl, media researcher; Kathy McColley, production specialist

Our very special thanks to Matthew T. Miller, Paleontologist in the
Department of Paleobiology at the National Museum of Natural
History, Smithsonian Institution, for his review. Capstone would also
like to thank Kealy Gordon, Product Development Manager, and
the following at Smithsonian Enterprises: Ellen Nanney, Licensing
Manager; Brigid Ferraro, Vice President, Education and Consumer
Products; Carol LeBlanc, Senior Vice President, Education and
Consumer Products; and Christopher A. Liedel, President.

Image Credits
Capstone: Jon Hughes, cover, 2–3, 6–7, 8–9, 14, 19, 20, 22, 29; Getty
Images: Ted Soqui, 24, ullstein bild, 25; Newscom: ZUMA Press/
Armando Arorizo, 27; Shutterstock: AuntSpray, 10–11, 15, 17,
18, 21, Catmando, 4–5, 30–31, Elenarts, 1, Esteban De Armas, 23,
hangingpixels, 7 (inset), Rich Koele, 5 (inset), roundstripe, 10 (inset),
Warpaint, 12–13, Zack Frank, 26

Printed and bound in Canada.
010814S8

TABLE OF CONTENTS

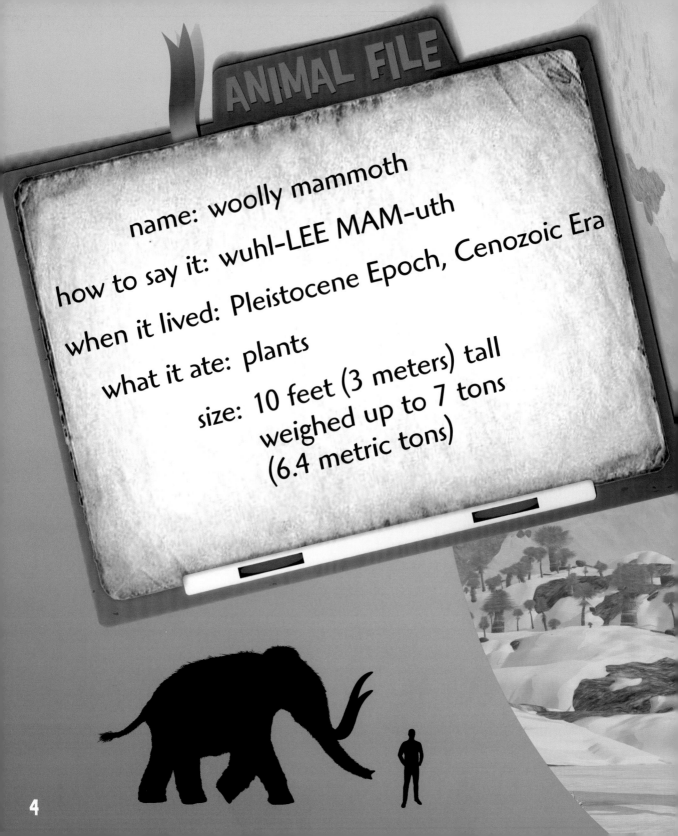

name: woolly mammoth

how to say it: wuhl-LEE MAM-uth

when it lived: Pleistocene Epoch, Cenozoic Era

what it ate: plants

size: 10 feet (3 meters) tall
weighed up to 7 tons
(6.4 metric tons)

Woolly mammoths belong to a group of animals called Proboscideans. Members of this group have long trunks and heavy tusks.

Thanks to FOSSILS

A fossil is evidence of life from the geologic past. Fossil bones, teeth, hair, and tracks found in the earth have taught us everything we know about woolly mammoths.

mammoth skull found in South Dakota

THICK SKINNED

Woolly mammoths had thick skin. Layers of fat beneath the skin helped keep them warm.

small ears

curved tusks

long trunk

Woolly mammoths are closely related to today's Asian elephants.

shaggy, furry hair

short tail

thick legs

HAIR, HAIR EVERYWHERE

The woolly mammoth's body was covered in two layers of shaggy hair. Even its ears were lined with hair.

The animal's long hair grew up to 20 inches (51 centimeters) long. The hair kept freezing rain and snow off the animal's skin. An undercoat made of shorter, dense hair was underneath the animal's outer hair. It kept the woolly mammoth warm.

Scientists believe a woolly mammoth's hair was light to dark brown. But scientists have discovered woolly mammoth fossils with red and orange-brown hair. This is because the animal's hair color changed after being buried in the ground for so long.

TOUGH TUSKS

Woolly mammoths are known for their long, curved tusks. These were made of ivory, like elephant tusks. Woolly mammoths used their tusks to fight one another and to fend off predators. They also used their tusks to dig in deep snow to eat the grass underneath.

People can tell how old a tree is by counting the rings inside. A new ring forms each year the tree is alive. Woolly mammoth tusks work in a similar way. Inside their tusks are rings and other markings. Scientists can tell the animal's age based on these markings.

The animal's tusks grew up to 15 feet (4.6 m) long. Each one weighed about 100 pounds (45 kilograms).

MIGHTY TRUNKS

A woolly mammoth's long trunk could reach up to grab leaves from tall plants. The animal also used its trunk to drink water. Water was sucked up into the trunk. Then the trunk blew the water into the mouth.

The woolly mammoth's trunk was strong enough to push heavy objects out of the way. But it was also gentle. Two fingerlike ends on the trunk allowed the animal to pluck bits of grass or flowers from the ground to eat.

A woolly mammoth's trunk could grow up to 6.5 feet (2 m) long.

A MAMMOTH-SIZED MEAL

Woolly mammoths were herbivores. They ate grasses, leaves, bark, and flowers. The animals used their wide, flat teeth to mash up tough plants. When a tooth fell out, a new tooth grew in its place. Woolly mammoths had a total of six sets of teeth throughout their lives.

Woolly mammoths spent much of their time finding and eating food. Their huge bodies needed plenty of food to keep moving. A woolly mammoth ate up to 450 pounds (200 kg) of food each day.

A woolly mammoth could produce 200 to 300 pounds (90 to 135 kg) of poop each day!

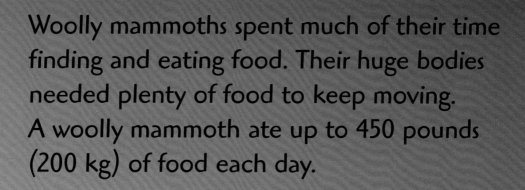

LIVING DURING THE ICE AGE

Woolly mammoths have lived on every continent except Australia and South America. They made their homes in grasslands.

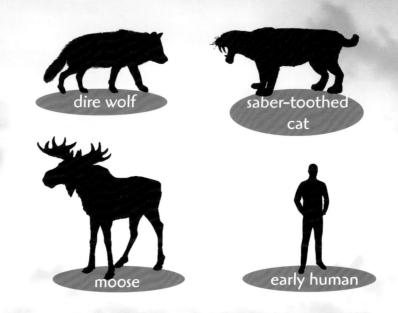

Other Pleistocene Animals

dire wolf

saber-toothed cat

moose

early human

The Pleistocene Epoch began about 1.8 million years ago. It ended 10,000 years ago.

CENOZOIC ERA		Pleistocene
Miocene	Pliocene	

20   15   10   5   0

Millions of Years Ago

These furry beasts lived during the Pleistocene Epoch. This epoch was part of the last Ice Age. During this time huge areas of land were covered in sheets of ice called glaciers.

STAYING TOGETHER

Woolly mammoths lived together in herds. The herds were made up of adult females and their young. Scientists know this because groups of woolly mammoth fossils are often found together.

Living in herds helped the adult females protect the smaller mammoths. Predators could attack young mammoths if they wandered away from the herd.

Male mammoths stayed in the herd until about age 10. As adults they traveled alone or with other males.

YOUNG WOOLLY MAMMOTHS

Woolly mammoths mated in late summer. The female gave birth to one calf about 22 months later. Woolly mammoths were mammals. Like other mammals, these animals gave birth to live young.

The woolly mammoth could live to about 60 years old.

Calves drank milk from their mothers. After a few months, calves would also eat plants. They continued to drink milk for two to three years.

PLEISTOCENE PREDATORS

Because of their size, adult woolly mammoths had few predators. Staying in the herd kept them safe from lions, saber-toothed cats, and dire wolves. Predators preferred to hunt injured or young animals.

Early humans were the woolly mammoth's greatest predators. Humans hunted woolly mammoths for meat. They used the skins to stay warm. Some scientists believe this hunting is what caused the animals to die out. Other scientists think the changing climate caused the woolly mammoths to become extinct. Warmer temperatures may have killed off the animal's food sources.

FOSSIL DISCOVERY

People had been finding woolly mammoth bones for many years. At first people thought the huge animals lived underground. Others thought the bones belonged to giant humans. Still others believed they were elephant bones.

Scientists dig up the fossils of a woolly mammoth in Moorpark, California.

Today scientists know more about the woolly mammoth than any other animal from the Ice Age. This is because woolly mammoths were preserved in the cold, Arctic climates. Complete woolly mammoths have been found frozen in ice.

a mammoth skeleton on display in Germany

FOSSIL SITES

Woolly mammoth fossils have also been found in Siberia and North America. In 1974 a huge fossil site was discovered in South Dakota. It's called the Mammoth Site of Hot Springs. Scientists have found the bones of more than 60 mammoths.

Some of the best-preserved prehistoric fossils have been found at the La Brea Tar Pits in Los Angeles, California. So far scientists have found fossils from 135 birds and more than 50 different mammals, including woolly mammoths, camels, llamas, and fish.

a mammoth sculpture at the La Brea Tar Pits

Scientists and volunteers continue to
search for fossils at the La Brea Tar Pits.

REDISCOVERING THE WOOLLY MAMMOTH

Scientists are learning even more about woolly mammoths with X-rays and CT scans. In 2010 scientists X-rayed the body of a baby woolly mammoth named Lyuba. X-rays of Lyuba's teeth and stomach helped researchers determine how old she was and how she died.

Some scientists think woolly mammoths will walk the earth again one day. Using a process called de-extinction, they hope to use blood and muscle tissue to recreate the animals. Scientists think a modern elephant could give birth to a woolly mammoth calf in the future.

"We could see for the first time how internal organs are located inside a mammoth. It's pretty important from a scientific point of view."
—Alexei Tikhonov, deputy director of
the Russian Academy of Science's
Zoological Institute

In 2013 scientists found a frozen woolly mammoth in Siberia. But this discovery was different from earlier finds. As they dug, scientists discovered the animal's blood was perfectly preserved. They plan to use the blood to learn even more about woolly mammoths.

GLOSSARY

climate—the average weather of a place throughout the year

continent—one of Earth's seven large land masses

epoch—an amount of time that is less than a geologic period and greater than a geologic age

extinct—no longer living; an extinct animal is one that has died out, with no more of its kind

fossil—evidence of life from the geologic past

grassland—a large, open area where grass and low plants grow

herbivore—an animal that eats only plants

herd—a group of animals that lives or moves together

ivory—the hard, white material of an animal's tusks

mammal—a warm-blooded animal with hair or fur; female mammals have mammary glands

mate—to join together to produce young

Pleistocene—the period of time beginning two million years ago and ending 10,000 years ago

predator—an animal that hunts other animals for food

prehistoric—living or occurring before people began to record history

preserve—to stop something from decaying

Proboscidean—a group of large mammals made up of elephants and extinct related species

trunk—the long nose and upper lip of an animal, such as an elephant, mammoth, or mastodon

tusks—very long, pointed teeth that stick out when the mouth is closed

undercoat—the short, dense fur underneath an animal's long fur

X-ray—a picture taken of the inside of the body

CRITICAL THINKING QUESTIONS

1. Woolly mammoths had long trunks and heavy tusks. Name an animal today that has similar features. Use the text to help you with your answer.

2. Woolly mammoths lived during the last Ice Age. Name two other animals that lived during this time.

3. Woolly mammoths are extinct. What does "extinct" mean?

READ MORE

Higgins, Melissa. *Woolly Mammoths*. Ice Age Animals. North Mankato, Minn.: Capstone Press, 2015.

Zeiger, Jennifer. *Mammoth and Mastodon*. 21st Century Junior Library. Ann Arbor, Mich.: Cherry Lake Publishing, 2016.

Zoehfeld, Kathleen Weidner. *Prehistoric Mammals*. National Geographic Kids. Washington, D.C.: National Geographic Society, 2015.

INTERNET SITES

Use FactHound to find Internet sites related to this book.

Visit *www.facthound.com*

Just type in 9781543505412 and go.

Super-cool stuff!

Check out projects, games and lots more at
www.capstonekids.com

INDEX